33

FIVERR

Power Tips

Featuring proven ways to
boost your sales and quit your job!

Check out these recent titles from us

Power Profits!

Power Profits! Cash Flow Revolution

63 Ways to DRIVE MORE TRAFFIC to your website

101 TOTALLY FREE ways to market your website or log

How To Build a YouTube Money Machine

The 10 Principles of ENDLESS WEALTH

About the author

Danial Barron Howe is the author of over 350 books ranging from business and online income to health and wellness. He is the founder of six multinational businesses including **2ndEmpireMedia**, the publisher of this book and FiverrPowerTips.Com a rapidly growing community catering to the ongoing education of the Fiverr community.

Dan has been involved in the information marketing business ever since he wrote his first book, ***POWER PROFITS!*** Nearly a decade and a half ago. Since that time he has gone on to sell over 750,000 books in both printed and electronic form as well as numerous audio, video and other hybrid forms of informational products.

In addition to his role as an informational product producer, he holds several degrees including a Masters in mechanical engineering and design as well as degrees in psychology and biomechanics. He is a lifelong tinkerer artist and visionary innovator with a passion for improving efficiencies of systems such as those found within this book.

Forward

Why would anyone get so excited about earning *five bucks*?

By now you have no doubt noticed that the Internet tends to pop up every year with another new idea on how to promote your website or make easy money. The latest "new idea" seems to be a trend towards ***micro job sites***. Many of these new sites have popped up in recent years but only one among them reigns truly supreme above all others – **Fiverr.com**

Founded in 2010, Fiverr is the 800 pound gorilla of micro job sites. In little more than a years time it seems to have come out of nowhere and exploded all over the net. At the time of this writing fiverrs membership is 20 million strong and growing with as many as 5000 gigs being added daily.

Should you get involved with fiverr?

Yes! With a membership pool this deep (and getting deeper every day) that represents a gold mine of opportunity just waiting to be harvested. It should be noted however as well that there are two major differences between a successful fiverr seller and one who fails:

1. The successful seller has learned how to identify a "*winning*" buyer group with a recurring user base.
2. The successful seller also has a streamlined system (based on templates) to get his work done in the fastest, most efficient way, *often in only a few minutes.*

I can't develop your listings for you, nor can I market them for you. What I *will do* is teach you how to discover winning gig ideas and get good at driving buyers to your sales pages. *Very, very good…* This above all else is what will separate you from those that never seem to seen any attention, despite having otherwise very marketable ideas.

Why most how-to books are out-of-date before they are ever written even published.
A lot of "*how to*" books are written by folks who got out of the business more than half a decade ago (marketing of any type is always changing and you need to stay on the cutting edge.) or by academics who believe they understand the "mechanics" of a business enough to teach others. Sadly, most do not!

Still, others are make it only because of the number of personal contacts in their *Rolodex*. These are the ones that tell you how they made a million dollars using their "*XYZ 3 step automatic plan*".

Oh, if it were only that simple! These old ideas won't work on Fiverr.

I am a full-time information marketer.
Let me be clear upfront; I am not going to fill your head full of theoretical nonsense or recycled gibberish that I've pulled from various places all over the Internet. *I am a full time professional information marketer and TOP RATED Fiverr user.* I'm in the trenches each day earning a living by the knowledge that I've acquired over a decade and a half of actual use. I have to, this is how I feed myself and my family!

… And now for a shameless marketing plug:
Although the information in this book will take you a long, long way in the understanding of setting up your own personal Fiverr sales machine, the tips found here are only a few of the many tools available to you and you should always be on the lookout for more. You wouldn't expect to build a house using just one hammer would you?

When you're ready to take your Fiverr sales to the next level, I've put together a virtual toolbox of Fiverr resources for you on my website. Inside you'll find:

- *Plug-and-play sales pages- All you need to do is just fill in your specific gig information and drop it into your fiverr sale page.*
- *You'll get the very same templates I use to lay out my sales with - You'll also be able to develop original, marketable & hugely profitable e-books for sale on fiverr, amazon and more in a matter of hours - not weeks or months.*
- *…and I'll even show you how to set up a fully functional website using a free development software package that comes complete with shopping cart, photo gallery and advanced tools!*

For more details on this product and many more, visit my site at:

www.FiverrPowerTips.Com

Index

Preface

What does it takes to make a living online?
When you look at the statistics for failed business startups the prospects are pretty dismal.
Why do so many fail? Generally the answer falls into three categories:

1. They are inadequately funded
2. The owners lack an essential skill or knowledge (or at the very least a workable plan)
3. But the biggest is *loss of motivation…* This happens a lot in the informational marketing business. And the same goes for Fiverr as well.

The good news is that gaining traffic for your fiverr sales does not have to take a huge upfront investment of cash or really even much effort either. It can be grown step-by-step-as I have done – and I will show you the best of everything I know right here in this book.

British Prime Minister Winston Churchill, famously addressed a graduating class. When asked to speak he stood up, walked to the podium, quietly surveyed the crowd in attendance and instead of delivering an expectedly long winded speech, he simply announced *"Never give up! Never give up! **Never <u>ever</u> give up!**"* and with that he returned to his seat…. nuff said.

Building a sustainable business on Fiverr is a numbers game.
It may come across as obvious to many of you, but understanding this fact is the key to success. The misunderstanding many beginners have is to expect to create *a single gig* that will produce a flood of traffic

year after year, and that thinking won't get you very far.

To be a successful you must have *many promotional hooks in the water* at any given time. Fiverr allows you to post a maximum of 20 gigs, and successful sellers know how to take advantage of all of them. Some will make you a little bit of money, while others could make you a lot!

The reality is that if you only put up a couple of gigs on Fiverr and expect the traffic to beat a path to your door you're going to come away sorely disappointed. As mentioned earlier, Fiverr is growing by leaps and bounds and its user base is currently in the millions. However, there's only so much room on the top page to be a featured seller. If you're not on that page it's unlikely anyone will ever know you exist. This presents a problem; *how will the buyers find you?* The answer rests solely on the actions that you take to actively promote your gigs on your own.

Relax, everything you need to succeed is already at hand.
Promotion of any kind isn't rocket science. You are simply finding relevant groups of interested people and letting them know where to find you (or maybe just making your first introduction.

Let me assure you that you don't need a sparkling personality or outstanding speaking skills. (Even when it comes time to make your promotional video) Heck, you don't honestly need the looks of a Hollywood actor and you really don't even need a great education. I've seen several successful examples of this theory all over fiverr! All you need to do is a little one time work to develop a well laid out, organized presentation and know how to deliver it in the most effective manner.

What DO you need most to be successful?

Volume! As I said before, success with Fiverr is a numbers game. The more you put yourself out there, the closer you come to greater and greater success as a seller. Don't worry, you WILL get there, but I won't try to kid you and tell you that it doesn't take an investment of your time and effort up front to get things moving. But, just picture yourself sitting on a tropical beach while the rest of the world deposits automatic money into your account from sales you made online. People do a lot more difficult things all over this Earth every day for the sake of a "job".

*(No doubt you've heard this "dream scenario" many times before but I can tell you **this is my reality!** Internet marketing has allowed me to move from America to an island paradise in the Philippines. As I sit here dictating this book I'm on the back deck of my house overlooking the ocean. Rough life eh?*

What if I do something wrong or nobody buys anything?

Don't worry, you'll screw up and you'll probably get involved in many unproductive activities more than once that will make you will want to quit and lick your wounds. It's happened to the best of us. Here's my best advice; *Get over yourself!* This is a learning process and nobody learns by succeeding all the time. If you picked the wrong gig offer, designed a horrible looking pitch page, or just lacked the confidence it takes to make a well presented audio or video, learn from it! Make the appropriate adjustments and then move on. Don't give up.

My secret:
Do you want to know a secret that few beginning Fiverr promoters recognize when faced with a situation like this? We live in the digital age. NOTHING ONLINE IS PERMANENT. Corrections can be made with just a few keystrokes and the click of a mouse. And you can always update or tweak your offer as many times as you want. New potential visitors will never know how bad things used to be.

Really, every time you develop a new gig offer you are beginning with a clean slate. Once you have learned the basics, then you'll have a *template* to work from. The truth; is there is no reason to be embarrassed or worry about ruining your reputation. Unless you are a well-known celebrity most visitors to your sale page could care less who you are, as long as what you're providing is of sufficient value to them.

The biggest mistake you can make.
The truth is; not every gig on Fiverr is worth a damn. No matter how amazing you may believe your offer is, or how snazzy the promotional video or associated photos look or even how slick your pitch is. Bottom line: Fiverr buyers vote with their wallets. If you're not making sales the problem is something you're doing is not resonating with buyers and if you fail to address this fact you will never hit the big time.

Often times fiverr sellers with no formal promotional skills jump headlong into ideas that they *think* the public would be interested in, never doing even the least little bit of research to find out if there *actually even is* a market. My advice here is simple: proceed slowly. Test things out with a few promotions (you have nothing to lose - it's always free to post your gigs) and see what kind of traffic comes of it before getting crazy and going all out.

The greatest system of the 21st century.
Throughout the course of my life I have been involved in many, many different enterprises. I have been a real estate investor, television producer, professional motorcycle manufacturer, and a whole host of other things. Each business came with its benefits and drawbacks however, few ever provided me the free time to actually enjoy my life the way marketing informational products has. The internet has truly revolutionized the way business can be done – *but if and only if you learn the rules first!*

I can say without a doubt that developing informational products and services and then marketing them through my various sales channels such as my websites, blogs, Youtube videos and yes, even fiverr as well has been an ongoing challenge and a thrill for me.

Sure, there was a learning curve with all of it, there always is. But, once I crossed that threshold into knowledge and proficiency I was able to enjoy a lifestyle that few will ever able to experience.

If you desire a life filled with more free time, the ability to apply your creativity in myriads of ways and a potentially far better rate of pay then you're currently earning, remember the words of Winston Churchill; *"Never give up! Never give up! Never, ever give up!"*

Ready? Then let's get started!

#1 Capture Your Buyers email

Fiverr has some rather draconian rules when it comes to speaking with your buyers outside of their environment. Effectively, if you're caught outright soliciting buyers to contact or do business you outside of Fiverr you'll first receive a one-time "slap on the wrist" and if it happens a second time you will be banned outright!

With rules like this it leaves one to wonder *"how could I possibly build a list of repeat buyers if I'm not allowed to make contact with them on an ongoing basis?"* It is food for thought, and it bothered me for a long time too. Thankfully, Fiverrs rules are not all they're cracked up to be and there are still a few *loopholes* in the system. You just have to know what's acceptable and what isn't.

I'm going to kick off this book by giving you the VERY BEST TIP FIRST. This one method alone could potentially line your pockets with hundreds, even thousands of dollars a month!

The best way to secure your buyers contact information is by <u>delivering your gigs via an auto responder such as Aweber</u>. Aweber is a full service email marketing system and the choice of top affiliate and information marketers all over the world.

http://bit.do/aweber-discount

If you're selling a gig that can be electronically delivered (and you should be) such as an e-book ,audio program or video tutorial, you can set it up to be automatically delivered to your buyer by Awebers system once your buyer has entered their email to gain access. The whole process is pretty slick and completely hands-off. Here's how you set it up:

- **Create your electronic product** then store it in a secure place on your site or server (access to it will be your *delivery file link*. It should be hidden from public access without anyone having direct access without having the link.) If you don't have a host yet you'll need one now– **see tip #4** for my top recommendations for the best hosting platforms

- ***Sign up to Aweber*** (use this link and you'll get your first 30 days free). Create a mail list and call it *Gig 1 Delivery*– Aweber has an outstanding tutorial section on their website and it's very easy to follow along to get things set up, so for the purposes of this explanation I will spare you taking up space for this step.

    When setting up your first email to your buyer it should include the *delivery file link* in the initial welcome letter (thereby completing your obligation to the seller)

    You will however, still need to manually send a simple thank you note to the buyer through in order to stop the internal fiverrs delivery countdown clock. That's not really a big deal if you do as I've done and set up your smartphone to receive emails from fiverr so you can take care of that small issue on-the-fly.

- Create a ***landing page and insert your Aweber email signup code***. You can set up a simple one-page WordPress landing page to welcome your buyer and thank them for purchasing your product as well as capture their email so that their product can be delivered and the automatic *sales funnel* process can begin. If you used one of my suggested hosts then any one of them will come with a free WordPress installation package as part of the plan.
  If you're totally confused at this point, don't be. I'll go over this one more time for you once I get through explaining the needed components.

- ***Go to Fiverr.com and write your gig listing*** - When you come to the listing section called ***buyers instructions*** be sure to put your link to the landing page you just created and let your buyer be ready for the fact they will need to enter their email and go to their email box to verify it before they will receive your product.

That's it! You have created a product and captured the buyers email in one *automatic swoop*. Let's take a look at how this works step by step so you can understand it in real time.

1. Your buyer views your sale on fiverr and decides to make a purchase

2. Fiverr sends them a notice that contains your **instructions to the buyer** and a link to your *landing page*.

3. Buyer clicks the link – and is taken to **the landing page** where he fills out his email and clicks the **submit** button.

   In step two the buyer was already informed that he was going to need to check his email to verify it after submitting his information (you could also choose to repeat this instruction as well on your landing page too – not a bad idea.)

4. Buyer goes to his email at this point and clicks the *"verify your email"* link that was sent to him by Awebers auto responder.

5. Clicking the verify link triggers Aweber to instantly release your **welcome email** containing your products **access link** to the buyer and with that, the process is complete and you have a new buyer added to your email list!

   *All you have to do now is remember to send a thank you note to stop the countdown clock.

#2 Build A Sales Funnel

In tip #1 you learned the basics of creating an email list using an auto responder to deliver the initial product. Now I'm going to show you how to maximize your new list of buyers by offering them additional items for sale at ever higher prices. In marketing terms this is known as creating a *sales funnel*.

So let's assume you have a nice list of buyers building up on a daily basis. *What else* can you do with this list? The possibilities are endless! We'll explore a number of good ones later on in this book, but for now I want to call your attention to the fact that by creating a mailing list you have set yourself up to become less dependent upon Fiverr to bring you random buyers. Once you have a sizable list of buyers with a proven record of spending money on your products, you can send out an email at any time featuring your latest offer and generate income literally *at will*!

It's a well-known fact that buyers who have done business with you are up to 10 times more likely to do so again as compared to a complete stranger. That's great news for you and your long-term prospects as a marketer. It's true what they say, *"The money is in the list!"*

As long as you continue to maintain a *reasonable amount* of contact and always remember to add value to the people on your list whenever you send them anything, they will stay with you year after year. I have some names on my lists over a decade old!

By now I have probably got you pretty excited about the idea of generating sales whenever you feel like it. I know once this became a reality for me it became tremendously liberating.

The key to maintaining an ongoing relationship with your email list is to not treat them like a bottomless pit of money that you can reach into whenever you feel like it. People don't like to feel like they're being constantly marketed to. For this reason I maintain a *4:1 message to marketing ratio*.

I try to reach out to my lists at least twice a week. Anything more tends to feel a little *spammy*. I'm respectful of the fact that people have other things to do with their life then read my marketing materials.

#3 Flooding The Funnel

The beauty of using Aweber for building your email
lists is in its ability to follow up on *automatic basis*. If
you are selling a product on fiverr you can craft a whole
host of related follow-up messages to your buyers that
can be time released offering similar higher-end
products found through endless affiliate offers available
around the net.

Example:

Let's assume we have a gig on fiver that offers a small
e-book we put together on *how to build a website*. We
know by the very nature of this purchase that our
buyers are likely interested in websites, website
creation and possibly anything to do with marketing or
products of a graphical design nature.

A quick look around at some of the top affiliate sites
comes up with a whole host of very profitable offers we
could weave into the conversation of a weekly sales
letter that would be automatically delivered by Aweber
once or twice a week.

We can offer things like:

- web hosting-profit $100
- graphical design software-profit $65
- deals on domains-profit $15
- WordPress expansion packs-profit $50
- marketing and promotion software-profit $125
- even consulting services with profits paid to affiliates for generating leads-profit $250

You can quickly see why moving your buyers off of fiverr and on to your personal lists as fast as possible can reap you some amazing profits incredibly fast.

#4 Establish a website or blog

Our goal is to get people off of fiverr and on to your website, blog and mailing list as soon as possible. To do that you first need to set up a website or blog to point them to. That being said, I cannot stress enough how important it is to select a quality host.

Dealing with bargain-basement website hosting providers is a sure recipe for disaster. You should go with a host and has a proven track record. I've used many different hosts over the years and without a doubt I can tell you very few of them have stood the test of time, with the exception of the three featured below:

BLUEHOST

STARTLOGIC

1&1 HOSTING

It is essential to have a host of won't *go down* when you need them. If your site is down when you're buyer goes to collect his purchase, you're not going to look very credible and it may even result in the buyer demanding a refund in hurting your feedback and seller stats!

Most so-called "cheap web hosts" often go out of business overnight or go down for days at a time without warning and wind up being far from a bargain in the end! Word to the wise: this is not the place to bargain shop. So, why risk it when quality hosting can be had for as little as $3.50 a month?

What else can you do with your website or blog?

You should consider your website or blog "marketing central". From here you can build additional mailing lists, post notices of new gigs you're offering on fiverr or even take suggestions for what gigs you should create next by taking polls from your visitors. No matter what else you choose to do with it, your site should contain a link back to each one of your gigs, acting as a kind of personal catalog of your offerings.

#5 Maximizing Your Seller Profile

Appearing alongside of every gig is a short blurb about you that you entered when you signed up. It's time to make some upgrades now so locate the *settings* tab and then choose the *public profile* option. Knowing exactly what to put in your profile description can be a great way to boost sales also if you understand how to use it correctly.

Currently fiverr has rules against putting direct links in your sale descriptions to anything outside its own site (with very limited exceptions will cover here in upcoming chapters) that rule does not currently apply to profile settings! That being said, it would benefit you greatly to sure there's a link to your website or blog found within your existing profile.

Tip: Sellers with long domain names or those who want to point visitors to a *subdomain* will be dismayed to discover fiverr has an annoying habit of wrapping their text around, leaving odd breaks in sentence structure. If you find this happens to your link in your profile description you may want to use an url-shortner such as **bit.ly** or **Goo.gl** to make it all come out on one line.

At the *bare minimum* your public profile description should include:

- A picture of you. People who like to know who they are doing business with so put a face on your name (and be sure to smile dammit! This isn't a mug shot.)

- A short description of your specialty (if you have one) ideally your collection of gigs should have a common theme so you're seeing is a specialist, not a Jack of all trades.

- A link back to your blog or website as outlined above. Ideally the page you point them to will have an email sign-up on it to get them on one or more of your mailing lists

#6 Maximize keywords

.

Here's an easy little SEO trick most folks overlook:
Most books on fiverr will tell you to search within the
top ranking fiverr sales to see what keywords are being
used. *That's limited advice*! A better way is to use
Google's keyword tool to seek out not only the best
keyword, but, find out how many people are searching
for it!

Think about this for second; if you find a popular
keyword on Google wouldn't it be equally as popular
on fiverr? Or if you find a keyword that doesn't
generate much traffic on Google isn't it reasonable to
expect you'll see *even less* on fiverr?

Learn to think like a search engine:

Taking this concept a little further, we can use Google's
keyword tool to help us pick the optimum title for our
Fiverr gig! (*You are aware that fiver gigs show up in
Google's search results from time to time aren't you*?)
Using this to insight our advantage creates the added
advantage of pulling in traffic from outside of Fiverrs
site directly to your gig!

Simple changes like this can make a massive difference
to your gigs visibility. While this tactic alone is not
enough to propel you to Fiverr fame and fortune, it is
part of a greater strategy that has a compounding effect.

#7 Don't Forget Your Video

Want to boost your sales by up to 220%? Put a video on your sales page. People love videos, and so does fiverr.com! Think of it as a byproduct of living in the YouTube generation or just a symptom of society's ever growing attention deficit disorder, but however you choose to look at it you can consider it *wildly effective!*

When you upload your sale photos you should also take the time to make an accompanying video explaining the details of what you're offering. It doesn't have to rival the latest Hollywood production or really even be that amazing it all, in fact you can even do a video using your cell phone provided it's not too shaky and the sound quality is not too dodgy.

If you're too self-conscious to show yourself on camera you could produce a motion capture video and simply speak over it as you display the graphics or you could even write out a basic sales script and go back on fiverr to hire someone else to do the on camera presentation for you.

A few things you should know about fiverr videos.

- Fiverr requires you to say *"exclusively on fiverr"* somewhere in your video – *evidently this must have something to do with their ongoing paranoia concerning the notion that anyone would do business that they don't get a part of.*

- Fiverr seems to have rules that they follow sometimes but not so much at others. I was told by one fiverr staff member that I had to appear on video. A quick look around at the thousands of gigs featuring videos will clearly demonstrate that is not the case. Could it be a policy change is coming? Hard to say. Just be aware that for the time being you can follow my recommendations above and be just fine.

- Fiverr videos are human reviewed, but not very well. On more than one occasion I have submitted videos and have been rejected for violations or omissions that did not exist. Case in point: I submitted one video three times before they finally noticed that I did in fact have the required *exclusively on fiverr* tagline within the video! -My suspicion is they are subbing this review work out somewhere in India so if you get shot down like me, you may want to closely review the rules and just resubmit again… *and again* if need be!

#8 Optimize Your Gig Titles

In tip #6 I spoke briefly about optimizing your page titles using Google's keyword search tool but for clarity let me expand on that topic a little more.

As I said earlier, a *perfect title* is one that's written for search engines and humans alike. These two objectives don't always see eye-to-eye. At the end of the day you're looking for titles that will capture your viewers' attention and get them to click on your sale link to read more.

For fun let's head over to Google.com and enter *any 'ol phrase that comes to mind* into the search box. Take a look at the titles of the websites that are in the top 10 ranking positions. Which ones are catching your eye and tempting you to click? Most are just basic and boring while others are merely a long list of keywords strung together. Some are good but most are just crap. This is a case of correctly optimizing your keywords for search engines but doing nothing for human viewers.

If you want to make the maximum amount of sales your gig titles must pull double duty and appeal not only to what search engines like, but what viewers want as well… and do it in less than 80 characters…no pressure!

Working within the tight parameters of fiverrs description requirements you are further restricted to using all lowercase letters, WITH THE EXCEPTION OF ONE WORD which may be featured in ALL CAPS. Knowing how and when to exploit this can profit you!

The intent of allowing one ALL CAP word is for the sake of *accent*. When writing your gig title pic the one word (often times it's a feature or benefit) that you would like to punch through and grab the buyers attention the most. For example:

I will PROMOTE your business or website
I will WRITE an article for your blog
I will give you my latest eBook one added BONUS book too

Notice how the enlarged word draws the prime focus to the core of the message? Often times buyers are skimming over hundreds of listings and this will help make the essence of your listing stand out in the flash of a second.

One more thing about gig titles that should be noted: Once you choose a gig title and submit it then that original title becomes part of the gigs url forever.

Should you ever choose to rename your gig (and you can certainly do that any time you like) you will still be stuck with the original gigs description as part of the link name. Ordinarily this doesn't present much of a problem but if for example your original gig was titled *I will submit your website to 500 search engines* and you decide to upgrade your offer to say, *I will submit your website to 900 search engines* it's likely to cause buyer confusion when he sees your link on a blog somewhere and finds something entirely different when he gets to your sale page. So my advice here is to be sure to get it right the first time…again, *no pressure!*

#9 Achieving Fiverr Top Page Displays

The surest way to gain the largest amount of traffic in the fastest period of time if to have your gig featured on the top display page of your gigs respective category. Getting there isn't easy, and it's a long way to the top and in the end, there is no guarantee of ever making it. Still, it's a very worthy pursuit because the traffic you can gain once you've made it can be staggering. Besides, even if you don't make it all the way up the mountain using these simple tips will put you well above the rest of the fray, and that will still translate to increased sales.

4 Keys to reaching top page ranking:

- ***Good ratings*** - This may seem like a *no brainer* but it's still none the less true. Fiverr counts on its sale pages to put its best foot forward to new and existing users. After all, they don't want to be guilty of "suggesting" a poor performing seller right?
  The key here is; keep those ratings up!

  There is nothing finer than a *perfect 100* score, but once you are in the game long enough somebody, somewhere will feel the urge to "*take you down a peg*". It happens. Just deal with it and move on. If you feel strongly enough about the injustice in your rating then take your case to fiverrs admins and they may just remove it.

  Losing your perfect 100 rating doesn't preclude you from making top page if your sales numbers are high enough however. I've seen a number of sellers ranked at 99 & 98% make it to the feature page. If you sink below this point however, you can forget ever getting a second look from fiverr (*or that case most buyers either*).

- *Huge sales* – It's really the old chicken and the egg scenario isn't it? People prefer to buy from sellers with a good feedback rating but you can't get feedback without any sales. This leads to the question: "*How can I break out of this cycle and entice buyers without any credibility?*" It takes time – *and the right bait*. As a newbie a sure fire way to draw in traffic is to give an irresistible offer – I cover this more here.

- *Be sure to have a video* – I can't say for sure as to wither having a video actually plays into a *ranking algorithm*, I asked but fiverrs admins were less than forthcoming with the inside scoop. Aside from that, you will be hard pressed to find a top page featured gig without one.

    Fiverr gives its sellers the opportunity to insert descriptive videos into their sales pages and goes to fairly big lengths to make that fact known. From this, we can safely assume a bit of favoritism is being shown to those that "*get with the program*".

- *Luck* - Sorry, I know you don't want to hear that, but it's true. Fiverr is a limited in its feature space with only a maximum of 94 possible category pages to be featured on, yet, it plays host to over 25 million members - all competing for the same attention!

The fiverr system *crams in* more featured buyers to its time space by rotating amongst the chosen few. This can give your sales some pretty wild *mood swings*. One minute you're on the top page, riding high on the tidal wave of buyers, the next you are no longer featured and sales fall flat as a pancake.

- My advice? Reaching top page won't happen overnight. When and if it does your stay there will only be brief. Enjoy the temporary ride and realize you are not in control of the traffic that comes to you by this method. Instead, focus on customer care, gain as much feedback from the traffic boost as you can and in the end that will carry you farther than anything.

#10 Ping Your Gigs

Once you have a gig posted on Fiverr you should let the world know about it in every way possible. One great way to spread the word fast is to *Ping the search engines.*

Without getting too overly technical, a *Ping* is a submission scheme that basically sends out little "notices" to an intended recipient - in this case search engines such as Google, Bing and others, and basically tells them *"hey! Look over here!"**

When you list your gig, fiverr does its own little "ping thing" to let the big guys know you're on board now, but that shouldn't stop you from a chance to self-promote!

You should be aware that there are literally thousands of other places you could ping your listings besides the big search engines. Of course digging them all out can be a real chore, so it's best handled by the use of specialized software made to do the dirty work for you. Most free sites do about 100 to 250 sites so don't get too excited. You get what you pay for.

Personally I use ***Blast-O-Matic.com Commander edition.*** It's a slick little app made to run off any android powered smartphone. With it you can hit over 150000 sites and save your computer power for more important tasks/

*Yes, I know there is a great deal more that goes into it than that but for our purposes here? Nuff said!

#11 Template & Automate
Whenever Possible

Time is money. We've all heard this expression, but nowhere is it perhaps more poignant than fiverr. Spending hours to complete a gig is no way to earn a living especially when you're making less than $4* a gig! Successful Fiverr users understand that it pays to create gigs that require less than 15 minutes to complete (thereby allowing them to knock out 4 jobs an hour - $4 X 4 pr. hour = potentially over $16 and hour…*much better!*)

Unless your clear objective is to use fiverr as a *loss leader* (in terms of invested time) for the goal of potentially drawing buyers into higher paying *off fiverr* jobs, It behooves you to stay away from any type of gig offer that can't be quickly replicated in mass.

Template your work

The best way to minimize your invested time is to create gigs that require simple *cut and paste* delivery - such as an eBook in pdf or doc form. Once you make a sale it's just a simple matter of copying your file into the deliver box and you are done.

Automate your work

Automation makes things *even better*. If you remember from the opening of this book how I set up an auto responder to get visitors on my mail list. This is automation at its finest! While you will likely never get things down to a completely *hands free* operation (within fiverrs system anyway) you should seek out ways to reduce personal involvement. This will free up your time for more profitable ventures.

* After paypal and fiverr take their cut.

#12 Article Marketing

If you've spent any time at all researching how to promote a website or blog, you have no doubt read that one of the BEST ways is through article marketing. I have discovered this technique works *even better* for fiverr gigs.

Let's say for example you are offering a gig to *design e-book covers*. You could submit a quick 600 word article talking *about the 10 most important things to remember when designing an e-book cover* to one of the many thousands of article directories all over the net and round out your article by providing a link for your readers that takes them directly to your fiverr gig!

Many of my readers have done this a number of times to great effect. Article marketing remains one of the most credible ways to promote a product or service without beating your buyer over the head with "*a hard sell*". Best of all, you're not limited to just merely one article, or one article directory. By creating a whole series of unique articles and pointing them all back to a few selected gigs you could create a massive explosion in your monthly sales!

.

#13 Drive Sales By Offering A Mini-Course

I love creating mini courses! The reason being is it accomplishes several things within one project.

- It establishes your credibility as an expert.
- It allows you to push additional up sells.
- It makes a great place to sell affiliate products
- It enables me to hold a viewers undivided attention for longer than a few minutes or an hour
- …and of course it gives you another opportunity to direct traffic back to your website.

Building your course may not be in all at once a fair either. I have used Awebers email auto responder system to set up courses on the daily installment basis. This installment process is also known as *drip feed* and I can allow you to hold your buyers attention for days and sometimes even months on end!

Suggest selling the first chapter of the more expensive course - then moving buyers off Fiverr to buy the rest.

#14 Sell Special Reports

Another great tactic that works just as good today as it always has is to write a free e-book or report (known as white paper) This is how I got my start of Fiverr. Your e-book should be filled with relevant information and of course should encourage readers to come back to your website or join your mailing list... *Or both!*

There are a number of different ways him to distribute your report. You could offer it in either popular format of pdf or doc file. When it comes time to deliver the product you could send them out manually but for maximum efficiency you learned my preferred method at the start of this book.

Producing your e-book or report need not be an expensive venture either. If you don't have Microsoft Word to put together your book then download www.OpenOffice.org (a freeware version of Microsoft's office suite that works every bit as good)

#15 Sell brandable reports & eBooks

Owning a blog or website is time intensive. Faced with a lack of time, it's not always easy for blog owners to come up with fresh content. Why not sell a collection of articles for buyers to use on their own websites or blogs?

Some sellers prefer to sell packs of articles with their own website or blog listed on the bottom with the understanding that these articles can be freely distributed by anyone who has them, however, their website must not be removed from the article. I'm here to tell you right now, that's never going to happen in a million years! Better to just sell the articles as nameless reports and let buyers put whoever's name they choose on them. As long as you capture the buyers email address. You will always have them in the sales funnel to sell them more later on.

Continuing with the brandable theme, why not create a brandable e-book, (Sometimes referred to as a *private label*), and allow other fiverr users to sell it? You can build the subject matter around things you can link to your personal affiliates and reap the benefits of someone else's distribution efforts. This can be a true win-win situation for both of you.

#16 Loss leaders & buyer momentum

When it comes to fiverr sales Replication is the mother of profit. Unique work takes time and that eats into profits that are slim to begin with. Should you ever offer complex or time intensive gigs? *Possibly...*

Years ago many large grocery store chains and big box retailers began experiments with customer behavior based on data collected over years of research. It was discovered there was a *97% percent probability* of a sale if they could just get the customer in the door. But how to do it? The answer came by playing to the consumers "greed".

No doubt you've seen the Sunday circulars offering future products at unheard-of low prices such as a 12 pack of soda for 1/3rd the normal going rate or two-for-one offers. These are called **loss leaders**. They are carefully crafted offers designed to get you off your butt and into the store. Once you're there, retailers are counting on the fact that you will use the opportunity to pick up more than just that one simple offer.

Buyer momentum

If you were in the store to pick up our soda offer from earlier, chances are you would likely think to yourself *"Is there anything else I need as long as I'm in here?"* That's the million-dollar question isn't it?! This one simple tactic is responsible for millions upon millions of dollars in retail sales each year. If it works for them - *it can work for you too!*

Take a minute to consider what kind of a gig offer you can put together that is so outrageous, so desirable or such an incredible bargain that your visitors simply won't be able to resist the urge to click that *buy it now* button.

Once you gain a sale you need to be ready with follow-up offer of a higher value. Of course not everybody will be a taker, but if you spend some time and put together a related follow-up offer that still contains a great value to your customer, the odds are on your side!

#17 Solicit Feedback

Fiverr sellers live and die by feedback. The fastest way to skyrocket sales is to have a solid feedback rating. Sadly half of all buyers don't bother to leave feedback and all, this represents lower perceived *trust rating* in the eyes of new perspective buyers - look at it this way: who would you give stronger consideration to; a buyer with a 50 feedback score or one with 100?

Unless you have your own system in place, staying in touch with your buyers long after the sale is difficult to do because fiverrs system is so ill-equipped for organized follow-up. That being said you can still remind your buyers to leave you positive feedback in one of two ways:

The Ethical bribe.
When I deliver any gig I make a point to deliver a *thank you script* along with my product or service delivery. Inside the script I encourage the buyer to leave the immediate feedback and offer them an *additional bonus* for doing so. This additional bonus can be a special report, a small related eBook I wrote or even possibly 500 more automated SEO submissions.*

The Email follow-up.
Did you build an automated email list? This would be a good time to use it! If your gig delivery system was set up in advance to use the email method I outlined in Chapter 1 then you should have a new subscriber receiving automated messages every few days.

In order to maximize automation and jog your buyers memory, I would suggest you put in a reminder to your buyer at about day five - along with an incentive such as I outlined above.

Whatever you do never demand buyers leave you positive feedback. Doing so is gaming the system and fiverr will not appreciate it one little bit. In fact they could get you kicked off. Simply solicit your feedback and trust the system. If you deliver value to your customer you have nothing to fear.

#18 Clone your gigs

Think about this for a second and you will see the wisdom in it, especially when you are struggling to come up with 20 *"completely original"* gig ideas.

Every fiverr seller can tell you that there are one or two gigs in their offerings that vastly outperform all the others. As for myself I have one that does 4 times the income of all the other 19 combined!

Why not copy your most successful gig and create a 2nd, 3rd or 4th listing? True, you'll have to *spin* them a bit to avoid relisting a straight up copy, but as of this writing fiverr seems to have no problem with this practice!

Cloning your gigs for bigger market share.
Herein lies *"the secret advantage"*: Let's assume you have a gig posted offering to design business cards. You post it and then begin burning brain cells looking for other tie in topics (or totally different ones) to add in for your remaining 19 listings. There is a better way to rack up listings and corner the market on business card exposure all at once…

Rather than move on to another segment all together, simply *tweak your listing* just a bit and relist it over and over– like this.

- I will **design you a killer business card** for $5

- I will **create a one of a kind business card** for $5

- I will **deliver a professional quality business card design** for $5

Same basic service, but totally different listing! By applying this little known technique you have *radically upped your odds* of being discovered when a buyer goes looking for someone to design a business card (or whatever your niche may be).*

As time goes on you will be able to watch your traffic stats and see which listing is getting the *lion's share* of attention. Meanwhile you could be researching other gigs to try out and perhaps delete your bottom 15 business card gigs and try a new gig posted in 15 different ways.

Wash-rinse-repeat!
Using this process is a terrific way to build up a powerful catalog of gigs. Sure, it will take a little time, but your efforts will be paid back immensely!

Also, **Be sure to use different key words in each listing as this will "spread out the net" a bit wider and offer a larger group of words to be discovered with.*

#19 Broadcast yourself

Youtube is the world's 2nd largest search engine. That being said, it's also one heck of a lot easier to get noticed on than its big brother, google!

There are so many good ideas you could incorporate Youtube into that all of them put together could make a book unto themselves! Here's the best of what successful fiverrs have shared with us:

1) **Mini videos:** Making a succession of dozens of tiny little 2 minute videos and packing them with related keywords is a great way to make it to top page on google. Did you know that happens? Try this: do a random search on google and you will usually always find videos amount the top page results. Reason? Google owns Youtube!

   It's a sneaky way to avoid weeks of SEO setup and it works like gangbusters! (to learn more check out this tutorial – complete with how to videos)

   Once you get your mini videos up and running point them all to your gigs and – booyah! Instant traffic!

2) **Repost your actual fiverr video.** Go ahead, why not? It's not like the listing is costing you anything for the additional exposure and the added benefit of a free Youtube back link certainly isn't going to hurt your chances with finding new viewers either.

3) **Vlog** – *aka Vlogging* is net speak for *video blogging*. If you can stare into the unblinking eye of a camera and coherently ramble about topically related subjects every so often, then you my friend have a POWERFUL platform to "suggest" your viewers check out your fiverr gigs!

#20 Develop a delivery package

Popular statistics repeatedly demonstrate that a buyer is *ten times more likely* to make a *second purchase* from someone they have purchased from before than a complete stranger, so why not use that to your advantage while your buy is still feeling the impulse to buy?

When delivering your gig you should have a "*thank you script*" prepared to deliver to your buyer at the time you turn over the goods.

This script can be saved in a simple txt file and then cut and pasted into the delivery box you use to send you buyer their product or service delivery notice. It should include a mention of any outside projects - such as a newsletter along with a direct link or at the very least a reminder of other related gigs.

Here's an example of a *winning script* that gets delivered when we do an SEO job:

Thank you for your order!

YOUR GIG IS COMPLETE! We have submitted your site and it will be indexing for the next 24 to 48 hours.

In addition I gave you a BONUS of another 1500 indexes @ NO EXTRA CHARGE

Want to learn how get more out of FIVERR? See our blog at http:FiverrPowerTips.Com

We at 2ndEmpireMedia we want to help you get THE MOST out of your promotional efforts.

To help you we have a FREE ONLINE DAILY TUTORIAL for you filled with tips, tricks and even some great tools to help skyrocket your marketing efforts. http://goo.gl/aQAKWj

If you're looking to grow your information or affiliate business to a new level we now offer website hosting packages that are quickly becoming the industry standard - starting as low as $3.49 a month!

http://whamtrade.com

Once again thank you for your business & we hope to see you with us again soon

2ndEmpireMedia llc

This one script alone has generated well over $25,000 a year in outside sales.

#21 Deal with negative reviews quickly

Besides blemishing a perfect track record and shaking buyer faith in you, bad reviews hurt your display rankings in fiverr too. As mentioned elsewhere in this text, Fiverr gives a higher priority to sellers with excellent feedback scores. Losing favor with fiverr means loss of potential top page display and that can also mean losses of potentially thousands in sales over a years' time!

While you can't always control a cranky buyer with a chip on his shoulder or someone who just is out to be an ass to everyone he meets, you can proactively appeal unjust feedback to fiverrs admins for removal consideration. I've done it a number of times myself and in each case the staff at fiverr has been quick to handle things and set my score right.

Many users don't take this tip seriously enough and suffer some unnecessary hits to their score. When you see something you feel you don't deserve – handle it quickly! You only get a short window of time to work things out. After that you're stuck with it. Taking a proactive stance to protecting your reputation can mean the difference between *superstar* and one who merely "also ran".

#22 Do Testimonials

If you set this up right you can not only get paid by you can even get FREE STUFF!

Whenever you read an e-book or newsletter or some product you find interesting take a minute to write a quick note to the author and include your website address. You might be surprised, this may be enough to get an easy back link when the author post your testimony on his website.

My personal belief is testimonies have lost their effectiveness over the years because it's too easy to fake an insincere one. For instance some may question the ethics of doing so but you can actually hire people to give you video testimonies on Fiverr.com. I've seen more than one information product with video testimonies embedded in it that obviously were made using this tactic.

My advice here is before you do anything like this make *absolutely sure* that your country's laws don't prohibit such activity. And remember; every single time you do something online. It builds or damages your reputation so think wisely before you do something you'll regret later.

#23 Be an Authority

People will pay for your advice. You could offer advice or critiques on all kinds of things.

The fastest way to become an authority is to just start talking! Join several forums within your niche and promote your site via your signature line.

Be careful. Always read and understand the forums rules concerning self-promotion. Some take a dim view of blatant self-promotion while others could care less. Be sure you understand what's permitted so that you don't annoy the forum moderators and find yourself getting banned.

It's a good idea to lurk around for a little while and see how other users are posting and how other site members react to it before trying anything on your own.

You also need to take note of the fact that many affiliate agreements specifically say that posting an affiliate link within a forum constitutes spamming. Ignoring this rule can get you booted from an affiliate program and you could wind up losing any commissions you've earned as well!

Slow and steady wins the race. Build your reputation as an authority by posting sincere, helpful and useful comments. Don't be in a hurry to plaster the entire Internet with back links to your site. The links will come on their own. All you need to do is come up with useful and relevant answers to the issues being addressed within the forum. If other members find value in what you have to say, they will automatically give you credit you deserve and respond by wanting to know more about you and your website without being asked to do so.

#24 Arbitrage

As big as fiverr is getting, it's still a relatively little known corner of the web. That can mean some big profits for those that know how to play the role of *middle man*.

I have a *love-hate* relationship with craigslist. As a seller I'm constantly disgusted when my listings get flagged within minutes and taken down *(most commonly by competitors and there is nothing you can do about it except to relist again and again!)*. However, as a buyer I've learned to find real gold, especially as an *arbiteaur**...

Welcome to the world of *fiverr arbitrage*.

Arbitrage *-in this sense-* is the art of finding a buyer in need and plugging in a supplier and pocketing the difference between the costs of supply and demand.

For example:

I recently combed through craigslist and found a number of potential help wanted ads looking for someone to set up a simple two or three page WordPress website and willing to pay up to $100.

Within 10 minutes of scanning fiverr I had come up with a list of 20 sellers offering the same basic service – and the price? Just $5!

Putting the deal together took about a hour total. I contacted the craigslist poster and took the job, jumped on fiverr, made a purchase and shortly afterward fired all my clients' server access info over to him. Within 1

day I received notice of completion back from my seller and I passed word to my client on the same day. Boom! $95.00 for basically about an hour invested.
Not too shabby!

If you think this concept is only something that looks good on paper but has a one in a million chance of ever happening, you are *DEAD WRONG*. This kind of thing happens every single day. Right now, somewhere, someone is paying a middle man for what he *knows*, not what he *does*. Knowing that fiverr exists (not everyone does) puts you in the unique position to *sub out* some incredible deals just like the one above.

* Don't look it up – I totally made the word up. But if it catches on just remember: you read it here first!

#25 Interact with your buyers

Putting a "face" on your business is a sure way to build customer loyalty. One way to do that is to take the time to interact with your customers through the feedback they give you.

Many sellers simply slap a rating on the buyer when asked to do so and move on to the next sale. This is a huge mistake! Potential buyers are checking you out. Part of what they see is your feedback. This gives the buyer a preview of what to expect when dealing with you.

Let's assume two equal sellers, one who takes the time to thoughtfully reply to each feedback in his que with comments like; *"Thanks for your business steve! It was a pleasure working on your project. Good luck with xyz!"* versus the other who merely gets the job done and responds with a blanket comment of *"thanks"*. Can you guess which one makes the most sales? Sure you can!

Go that extra mile with a personalized comment and you'll not only woo more buyers, but you'll set the tone for a much better experience with them as well!

#26 Be your buyers advocate

Going above and beyond starts by paying close attention to details. Perhaps there is something your buyer may have overlooked. You can be their *hidden asset* by spotting a mistake, an omission or future potential problem and calling it to their attention while gaining tremendous credibility with your buyer.

Say for example you were to offer a typesetting gig. If you were to spot misspelled or poorly punctuated sentences and call it to your buyers attention, there is little doubt the appreciation would be great. Not only that, it's unlikely your buyer would look elsewhere the next time he or she needed a similar service. Why would they when they would feel like they have a seller that has their best interest at heart?

#27 Blog Daily

With the advent of WordPress you can now create a blog extremely easy without even knowing how to program HTML. When you put up new gigs on Fiverr you can mention it in your blog giving a link directly to it.

It's a good idea to make friends with other blog owners too and when possible trade links with them. Here's a few good tips (**http://bit.do/fiverr-tips1**) on how to increase the likelihood that someone will want to link to your blog posts and swap

The ping is the thing!
When you post a message in your blog, WordPress automatically sends out a "*ping*" to the search engines to let them know you have just updated your site. It's a tremendously efficient system that doesn't require you to go out of your way to promote the work you've just done. It's all taken care of for you with the click of a button! Learn more about pinging here.

Additionally, services such as feedburner.com let your blog's feed be distributed effortlessly to each of your site's users. Plus they allow email subscriptions to your feeds as well.

#28 RSS feeds

RSS stands for "really simple syndication" and it's a form of standardized web feed format used for distributing content from blog entries, news headlines and a multitude of other sources.

Some readers will visit your blog to read it, others will opt to use an RSS reader from their computer or web-based service such as the one provided by myYahoo!

You can make it really easy for everybody who visits your site to subscribe by adding a handy little RSS, XML or myYahoo! Button to your sites blog. Many websites have at least half a dozen or more of these little special-interest graphics tacked onto their blogs. You no doubt have seen many cases of this, the more popular ones are Facebook, twitter, YouTube, G+, LinkedIn, Tumbler, Pinterest and more.

If you would like to learn more about RSS integration you can learn more in this video.

#29 Participate in blogs

Participating blog discussion is a time-honored link creator. Unfortunately, too many people have distorted this great resource by polluting the conversation with spam and off-topic junk or even going so far as to create entirely junk blogs just for the purpose of building their link profiles.

That being said, there are still several quality blogs to get involved with where you can promote your fiverr gigs. Correct blog participation involves being a part of the discussion without jumping on every opportunity available to insert a link or hijacking the conversation. When the time is right, insert your link.

Generally speaking, it's a good practice to build a reputation within a blog community before ever trying to post any links whatsoever. You don't want to become known as someone who only joined the blog for the sake posting his or her personal spam.

#30 Post Gig Links In Yahoo! Answers

Another great way to begin your ascension to Fiverr top ranking status is to get involved with Yahoo answers. People post questions on all sorts of topics and anyone can get involved in answering questions posed.

The asker and other readers can even vote on a particular answer as *best answer* and give it special prominence. This provides an opportunity for you to establish yourself as an expert.

You have to be careful about using irrelevant links in your answers as this is generally frowned upon. However if the situation calls for it and it is *absolutely relevant* you can provide links back to one of your gigs. When done correctly this can be a surefire traffic builder!

#31 Set Up A Podcast

Podcasting is really hot right now. If you don't podcast is think of it as an audio blog that can be distributed by RSS feeds or downloaded directly from your site to be played on any iPod, computer or MP3 player.

Visitors can subscribe to your podcast by way of RSS feeds and have it automatically delivered each time you complete a new show.

Podcasting can allow you to reach out to the world and connect with local new audience and the price is extremely cost-effective. I even produced a podcast from my bedroom office using equipment I bought from Amazon it does an amazing job for me with excellent sound quality and I've never wanted for more.

The goal is to hit the big time and get listed in as many podcast directories as possible. One of the best is podcast.net . Make sure your listings title graphic is bright and eye-catching so people looking through the directories won't miss you.

The added advantage of a podcast is they can always be saved and repurposed for other things. With a little editing and the right basic content you have the makings of an information product that can be sold from your site for added income!

Additional benefit is you could record interviews and sell them as products!

#32 Watch Out For Fads Or Go Evergreen

Chasing new fads and hot topics can result in some pretty huge payouts. A few fiverr users I know like to monitor popular television shows and track the latest news items. Once a hot topic begins to catch fire they create a new tie in gig as fast as they can or a blog or even a whole new website discussing the new product or fad and tie in an affiliate offer to monetize their efforts.

I'm personally not one for chasing fads. I prefer to only pursue the popular but steady types of trends whose popularity remains high year after year. These are referred to as *evergreen topics*.

The advantages of evergreen topics are the ability to put up a site or page and not have to update it or watch it so diligently, yet they continues to draw traffic month after month, year after year.

#33 Social networking (The "anti- tip")

No book on promotion could ever be complete without at least a mention of social networking. Sites like Facebook & Twitter dominate the marketing discussion but I have to question; "Are they really the best use of your time?" For fiverr promoters the answer would clearly have to be "NO!" People don't join sites like Facebook and Twitter to be marketed to. They are not in a buying mode. So in my mind they can never be considered a targeted group.

If you have ever taken even the slightest stab at using social media to promote your gigs and had little if anything to show for your efforts then then deep down in your heart you already know this is true.

At this point in the book you've been exposed to many other ways than social networking to get the word out and draw that traffic back in. I believe society has a tendency to be attracted to *shiny new things* and reject everything else as "*old-school*". Currently social networking has become the latest prime buzzword and promised *cure all* for business and website promotion - for better or for worse.

Don't get me wrong, social networking has its place. Sometimes it does in fact work. Most often it doesn't! It is not a *one size fits all* solution! Just as with any public forum the key here is to stay relevant to the pre-existing conversation. Don't attempt to hijack existing conversations or spam large groups of people with irrelevant links to your site. That tactic won't see you last very long and will likely get you kicked off.

Bonus Material:
Super charge your sales with affiliate offers

This bonus section is about finding related things to upsell to your existing fiverr buyers email list.

I'm a big fan of affiliate programs The beautiful part about them is there is never any upfront investment on your part and there's always something new coming out. Because of this, there is always something you can find to in tie into your latest promotional project.

It's generally a good idea to be a member of several affiliate programs at once. That leaves your options wide open and provides you multiple streams of income potential too. Just be sure when picking an affiliate or network to represent that it has a good track record for product support and payment. You don't want to be associated with a bad product or worse yet, have all your promotional work to go to waste and wind up never getting paid.

Some of the top affiliate networks are:

CJ.com

clickbank.com

Amazon.com

eBay.com

This is just a short list. If you'd like to see a few more click here

There are literally hundreds, if not thousands of others. Again, just be sure to do your homework before getting involved with any company. Your livelihood depends on knowing who you are doing business with.

Cross-link your other websites

Lastly, I want to share one of my personal favorite strategies for business growth, and that's *cross-linking all my efforts together*. This strategy goes deeper than merely linking websites. Actually, everything you do should link to *everything else* you do.

For example:

- your business cards should give your websites addresses and your blogs too

- your blog should link to your website

- your website should link to your blog

- if you have a brick-and-mortar store you should be promoting your website and blog

- your website or blog should be promoting your brick-and-mortar store

- if you do a podcast you should make mention of your website in your blog

- of course the blog and website should link to the podcast

- everything you do should push buyers to fiverr and fiverr should push back

- bottom line: every post you do should link to something else within your sphere

Where to go from here

I remember years ago when I got into internet marketing. I was overwhelmed by the sheer volume of information that I had to absorb. It seemed insurmountable! I quickly learned to take all these ideas in smaller chunks, implementing them one at a time. Which is why I wrote this book the way I did.

"The journey of a thousand miles begins the first step" in the famous saying goes. There's no right or wrong way to get started but the most you *can do* is to actually do it! Start at the beginning of this book and work your way through each of the ideas. Put them to use and test the results (measured in traffic and sales - that's the only *true* way that matters).

Spend each day taking another step and building another skill. I've been at this since 1992 and when I look back at all I have learned and accomplished since then I'm blown away by how much I've learned and managed to do with my daily addition of knowledge!

Now it the time to take your first steps. If you feel like I've been of help to you I'd like you ask you one small a favor in return;

Please take a moment to leave a positive rating for this book with Amazon so that others will be able to benefit from it as well.

See more recent titles from us

Power Profits!

Power Profits!
Cash Flow Revolution

63 Ways to
DRIVE MORE TRAFFIC to your website

101 TOTALLY FREE ways
to market your website or blog

How To Build a YouTube Money Machine

The 10 Principles of
ENDLESS WEALTH

For our full catalog visit us at:
2ndEmpireMedia.Com

www.ingramcontent.com/pod-product-compliance
Lightning Source LLC
Chambersburg PA
CBHW070910180526
45168CB00005B/1991